PRESIDENT THUG

HOW THE FATHER OF 45,000 LIES FLEECED,
FINAGLED, PHISHED, AND FOOLED FRIENDS,
FLUNKIES, FAWNERS, AND FOLLOWERS INTO
THE FIERY FLAMES OF DANTE'S INFERNO -
DONALD TRUMP'S OBSESSION WITH HELL

GARRARD MCCLENDON

Wayman Dean Press

President Thug

How the Father of 45,000 Lies Fleeced, Finagled, Phished, and Fooled Friends, Flunkies, Fawners, and Followers into the Fiery Flames of Dante's Inferno - Donald Trump's Obsession with Hell

Wayman Dean Press

P.O. Box 1073

Chicago, IL 60690

FIRST EDITION

Cover design and illustration by *Konee Rok*

ISBN-13: 978-0-9968832-4-5

eBook ISBN-13: 978-0-9968832-5-2

Library of Congress Control Number: 2020921861

McClendon, Garrard O., 1966 -

1.Politics. 2.Poetry. 3.Political Science. 4.Biography. 5.Presidents & Heads of State. 6.Government. 7. Executive Branch. 8.Political Leaders 9.Religion 10.United States - Racism. 11.United States - Race Relations. 12.Sexism. 13. Trump, Donald. 14.Presidential Biography.

❀ Created with Vellum

Media coverage of Donald Trump may eclipse that of any single human being ever. He has taken up semi-permanent residence on every outlet of any kind, political or not. He is no longer just the message. In many cases, he has become the medium, the ether through which all other stories flow.

— FARHAD MANJOO, NEW YORK TIMES

CONTENTS

FOREWORD

Every individual will be held accountable for their actions, in this life and the next. That is the message in Garrard McClendon's book, *President Thug*. The work serves as a repudiation of Donald Trump, but also signals a warning to traitors and liars.

For 15 years, Garrard and I have shared strong opinions and philosophies on changing the world. He has always questioned the status quo. In *President Thug,* his editorial offers a clever comparison and contrast of President Donald Trump's actions and his self-inflicted *Circle of Hell*.

The depths of malfeasance, with Trump's moral perversion and depraved indifference, beg for a side-by-side to the 700 year-old masterpiece, *The Divine Comedy - Dante's Inferno*.

An allegorical descent into the sin's of man, Dante's journey is frightening and McClendon's philosophical musings are poignant. Trump is a cult figure, inspiring devotion and a loyalty to emptiness and heartlessness. *Trumpism* is religion. His tendency to betray is pervasive, causing loyal associates to fall for the obvious.

Trump's garish gift of *reality-styled* politics constituted the definition of greed. His cruelty, mayhem, and dog whistles cannot be overstated. Instead of governing, he hunted enemies. But the crème de la crème of his maniacal proclivities surfaced when he offered to pay the legal fees for a man sucker-punching a protester at a campaign rally.

But there seems to be a special place in Dante's metaphorical Hell for *President Thug*. He has lied over 45,000 times, cheated, stolen, and tricked the American public into his shadow of sham and shame.

Writers should tread lightly before ascribing the worst criticism to another person, but *President Thug* shows Trump's shocking, inevitable, and disgraceful descent into the depths of Dante's Inferno.

—— Stanley G. Robertson, J.D., D.B.A.

ABANDON ALL HOPE YE WHO ENTER HERE

D ante Alighieri's *The Divine Comedy* still holds relevance centuries after its creation. The poem positions itself as a window and mirror to those who want to visualize the consequences of eternal damnation, the floating spiritual existence of a benign and anticipated purgatory, and the rewards of blissful paradise. But *The Divine Comedy* in a world of Donald Trump is a *Dreadful, Hellish Tragedy*. Dante begins by foreshadowing the city of woe and eternal pain. *Dante's Inferno* describes the delivery of punishment to willful, careless, and whimsical transgressors suffering torturous tumult. The bold and unapologetic malefactors must endure these consequences.

Dante's Inferno is a vision of Hell and how one

politician has demonstrated the selling of his soul on 9 levels, including seven capital sins. The president convinced over 6000 employees, public officials, friends, and acquaintances to sell their souls for fame, prosperity, and power. Soul selling defines the United States under multiple oppressive parameters during the Donald Trump administration.

If you have submitted to the wiles of thugs and have entered the circle of Donald J. Trump, your fate, reputation, trustworthiness, ethos, pathos, and logos will suffer horrid damage. Citizens of the United States, with the help of Russian operatives, persuaded the vulnerable to elect a heartless and evil person. What's more? He cheated on taxes, wives, friends, businesses, and banks, while boldly and erroneously claiming to be a billionaire.

Dante and Virgil's journey is child's play compared to Donald Trump's venture into Hell. Writing a narrative of President Trump's trespasses would be a laborious task, so just a few will be revealed.

Abandon all hope if you enter the *lair* of the liar. He is Beelzebub, the Lord of the Flies and Lies, Iblis, the Demogorgon, Mephistopheles, Prince of this World, but henceforth named, ***President Thug***.

Who would violate and denigrate tenants just

looking for a place to live? Donald Trump. The Trump Management Corporation was sued by the U.S. Department of Justice, for violating the Fair Housing Act. President Thug has a notorious propensity for belittling everyone. But his contemptuous hatred toward African Americans led him to refuse vacancies at his properties. Trump was sued for steering "undesirable" citizens to apartments far away from his properties. President Thug conceded and ate crow in 1975 by signing an agreement to not discriminate against Black renters, but he didn't admit to previous transgressions.

Hearing the word "thug" as a child, I knew there was a criminal and bad-natured element to the term. I surmised that anyone called a "thug" was violent, pitiless, and harmful. The definitions say it all:

Thug: 1. a violent or brutish criminal or bully. A brutal thug.

Thug: 2. a member of a group of murderers.

Thuggery: a noun depicting such behavior.

Thuggish: An adjective describing the behavior of brutal thieves.

Synonyms: *ruffian, gangster, goon, hoodlum, mobster, roughneck, monster.*

President Thug unmistakably fits the descriptions above. He is both crude and cruel. President Thug is a white supremacist, a racist, a sexist, an individual who believes and internalizes his "supposed" superiority, in turn, externalizing into actions that oppress, repress, suppress, and depress those he considers inferior or a threat.

His *oppression* delivers an offense that burdens his opponents with cruel restraints, harsh exercise, and vicious authority. His acts of *repression* keep others under control. His *suppression* wants to put an end to activities of persons or ideas in opposition to his, while his ultimate goal is that all three of these actions would *depress* the objectors of his philosophical and tangible goals. He is neanderthal, housing primitive notions of those who appear different or oppose his small-minded point of view.

President Thug is a sexist who has no regard for women, other than those who obey and pleasure him. He visualizes himself and the women in his sphere as trophies to be collected, dramatizing the lifestyle of a philanderer, who on occasion has a semblance of matrimonial verisimilitude. Women have collected him and he has collected them, like a dance of mindless magnetic mannequins in a meretricious, metallic store front. Being used and using are synonymous to him, because he doesn't care to know the difference if it benefits his short term satisfaction.

The game of politics is riddled with inconsistency, trick-shooting, unscrupulous favors, ebullient kindness for wrong reasons and storm cloud rudeness for right ones. Politics, though a strange bedfellow, can accomplish the highest good in a democratic society. But when a bedfellow cheats taxpayers, flaunts infidelity, fudges, and connives, the dismissal of a democratic point of view becomes evident.

When magicians and illusionists create a world of fantasy, the spectator is more than complicit in the trick. Making the elephant disappear or cutting a person in half only happens if the circus observer first believes the trick will happen. President Thug knows this. He knows that you need a box, an attractive person, a shiny simulated blade, a fast talking magician, and lots of noise and misdirection to believe that a woman can be separated at the waist without harm and then restored to complete the trick. He knows that gullible Americans, who frown upon science and reason, flock towards believing anything that may satisfy their unsatisfied groundhog days of discontent. He knows what wins the day: propaganda and sleight of hand.

President Thug has been around long enough to know that he has been enabled to do what others could only dream of doing. He's chemically coated like Teflon. Non-stick. If Presidents Biden, Obama, Bush (W.), Clinton, Bush (H.W.), Reagan, and Carter did the same things, they would have been run out of office immediately. Any other president would have been a 25th Amendment recipient with just cause for removal. He knew that he could cause more damage than Nixon because he had a whole party willing to fall on the sword for him. These are the malevolent MAGA minions -- the angry apologists that gave President Thug the benefit of doubt every time he committed illegal and nefarious acts.

The Daily Show's portrayal of President Obama's actions were child's play compared to President Thug's sins. President Obama's tan suit was a scandal. His lack of a lapel flag pin was scandalous. Having a hamburger with Dijon mustard was scandalous, but President Thug was praised for eating pizza with a fork. President Obama was criticized for not wearing a suit jacket in the Oval office, although Reagan had done it several times. Obama was ridiculed for taking pictures with a selfie stick, while President Thug received little criticism for posing, primping, and pimping for photographers at St. John's Church after turning security forces on peaceful protesters.

Long before the days of "The Apprentice," President Thug worked his wizardry on unsuspecting marks who were enamored with the shiny trinkets of his so-called riches. Gold toilets and prime real estate were his smokescreens for living life as a rich, "want to be" playboy. But having a "side wife" and "side girlfriends" made him palatable to those who longed for the womanizer to have matrimonial bliss and family life. He played that hand, later shattering expectations of fidelity towards business, friends, and women. Nihilism may be a temporary fix, until a nihilist takes advantage of you. Believing life is meaningless dishonors your own existence and the lives of others.

As they stroll, Dante and Virgil have a difficult time keeping the attention of President Thug. He wants to see all the Circles of Hell at the same time, not knowing that Inferno requires contemplation and the possibility of never getting to Purgatorio and Paradiso.

Thug likes saying the word "Hell," but doesn't comprehend being there. President Thug is a loose cannon who doesn't manage emotion. There are levels to Hell, and President Thug has achieved the unenviable goal of reaching every menacing level with his calculated and careless behavior. Sadly, President Thug has embraced *Limbo, Lust, Gluttony,*

Greed, Wrath, Heresy, Violence, Fraud, Treason, Pride, Envy, and Sloth.

The curiosity of the Trump presidency is in the way he chose to govern by distraction. Navigating without a compass, his leadership was haphazard at best.

"Are we going north? I don't know. Are we close to landing? Not sure," exclaimed Trump.

The Thug Presidency was a dance card with names shuffling so turbulently that dizzy dance partners staggered in a ballroom of confusion, not knowing when the songs began and with whom to dance?

You judge a person by accomplishments, character, and by those things the person never did, but claimed to have accomplished. You can also judge a man by his motivation to tout falsehood -- the characteristic of insecurity. He and his followers tell lies for gain and sometimes they lie just to lie. MAGA believed these lies and President Thug continued to drone the chorus, "My name is Legion, for we are many." He knows he is the father of lies.

Bob Woodward's books exhibit the "microscope and microphone" analysis of a POTUS who desires chaotic attention. Mary Trump's book shows us the realism of negative dynamics in the Trump family.

Tony Schwartz's book highlights the narcissism of a man who wants to take credit for all great things, deflect negative qualities, and parade a lifestyle of wealth beyond comparison. Michael Cohen's book takes us into the cave and internal chambers of financial and legal mischief and malice.

Prior to Thug's presidency, he built a fortified foundation of hatred and dishonesty. Sometimes failing hotels suffering from bankruptcy fall not because of mismanagement and questionable impropriety. They can meet their demise for defying basic hospitality, a questionable reputation, an undesirable location, or a lack of cleanliness. When he owned casinos, President Thug flippantly disregarded and squandered the gaming and hospitality professions. Trump flew into Gary, Indiana, on his private jet and pledged to make Gary a city that would return to glory with a riverboat casino on a lakefront with shuttered factories. Ten years later, Thug's company declared bankruptcy, leaving behind lawsuits and hard feelings in the majority-black city (Tareen & Biesecker, AP). He was no better with casinos on the east coast, which were sold, closed, demolished, or re-named.

Imagine African American employees being forced to disappear when Trump, his family, friends, and clients arrived at a property. Trump despises Black people. His fear and loathing don't present a good look. This discrimination case was in October 1973 in the United States District Court for the Eastern District of New York (U.S. v. Fred Trump, Donald Trump, and Trump Management Inc.). "The defendants, through the actions of their agents and employees, have discriminated against persons because of race in the operation of their apartment buildings, among other ways, by: Refusing to rent dwellings and negotiate for the rental of dwellings with persons because of race and color, in violation of Section 804 (a) of the Fair Housing Act of 1968."

Never wanting to admit guilt, he signed an agreement in 1975 to not discriminate against renters of color (Kranish and O'Harrow, Jr., Washington Post).

This is just the tip of the iceberg for the man who believes only in himself. He is the prince and power of the airwaves. You cannot escape President Thug. He is in the oxygen, so hold your breath.

Beware President Thug and Abandon All Hope Ye Who Enter Here.

2

LIMBO - I DON'T KNOW WHAT I WANT
CIRCLE OF HELL 1

The First Circle of Hell is the largest -- wide, spacious, almost never ending in its expanse. So vast, that its acreage can be a symbol for the excess leisure of not making decisions. This circle is not like those below it. There are no terrors, fires, slings, nor arrows in Limbo.

Those unable and unwilling to make hard decisions with the obligation of helping others, reside in Limbo. This is the level where mortals refused to be hot or cold, left or right, good or bad. Limbo is littered with inconsistency and cowardice, traits of those souls suspended in the acrylic of inaction.

President Thug feels relatively comfortable with Limbo because he feels he has never sinned -- he doesn't believe in right or wrong. His merits are based on what he judges as good for him. Later, in the Fifth Circle, he ridicules evangelicals, but here, he gets a pass because he admits to having no definitive belief or denomination. He alludes to being a Presbyterian, but he doesn't know anything about Reformed Theology, John Calvin, John Knox, confessional practices, Presbytery, the Apostles' Creed, or "The Book of Order." He doesn't acknowledge a reverence for a Creator and he's ignorant of traditional Christian practices including baptism, the sabbath, body and blood, recognition of the Crucifixion, and the importance of the Holy Bible. Unlike Dante, President Thug leaps into Inferno chasing fame, fortune, and love of self. He doesn't care about fighting Satan for the soul of Beatrice, or Ivana, Marla, or Melania. He only cares about self preservation.

Limbo turf offers the luxury of not having to apologize for white supremacist behavior, while former President Obama had to denounce his own pastor, the Reverend Jeremiah Wright from the Trinity United Church of Christ. The terrain in Limbo is wishy-washy, slushy, slippery, and unstable with potholes and pockets of mush. Here, your wife can start an anti-bullying campaign, yet you can be the biggest bully.

In Limbo, the atmosphere is more of an anti-punishment. Those born before Jesus Christ are here. The unbaptized are here with all of the "decent" people too. Noah built an ark and Moses parted seas. They were good guys, but don't get instant salvation. While in Limbo, you must hope for Purgatorio or Paradiso, but you can't get that without a visa from Minos.

Limbo is like a staging area or waiting room — Low Calorie Hell or "Hell Light." Dante says, "our sole punishment is without hope to live on in desire. Deep sorrow crushed my heart because both men and women of great worth I knew to be suspended here in limbo."

Limbo is the latin word for *limbus* meaning on the edge or the hem. This area is for those who are not saved even though they did not sin. Virgil advises that there are two categories of souls in this first circle. He says,

> "They did not sin: yet even their just merits,
> Were not enough, for they lacked baptism,
> The gateway of the faith that you profess.
> And, if they lived before the Christian era,
> They did not worship God in the right way."

Homer, Horace, Ovid, and Lucan are here, so President Thug feels honored to be among the poets. But since classical studies and the skills of reading and thinking aren't his strong suits, President Thug dismisses boredom, looking for a greater challenge in the next circle. He is comfortable, yet irritated with the lack of excitement.

Horrible people with unforgivable actions don't reside in Limbo. Virtuous pagans are the good people who didn't benefit from knowing the teachings of Christ. Although Paradiso is desired, those in the f*oggy* Limbo have eternal separation from the glory of Heaven. The sounds in the dimmer Limbo are moans and whimpers of sadness. In the more optimistic and brighter Limbo, Virgil explains,

"Their distinguished names
Which yet re-echo in your world above
Win for them heaven's grace which furthers them."

President Thug is drawn to the brighter Limbo, but still isn't satisfied. He longs for attention and excitement. During riots and protest scuffles, Thug doesn't blame himself nor does he condemn any person or entity that may affiliate with his base. Instead, he will blame everyone else. Scorched earth is his desire, as long as the forest fires blow away from him. "If I can't win, then I'll take my ball home, then nobody can play. There are some very bad people on both sides."

When not being obnoxious, President Thug straddles fences. This keeps his supporters happy and the persuadables from being disgusted with his crude way of communicating. Thug said that the United States of America doesn't have any more room for immigrants. He said the country was full.

"We don't want people coming here," Thug utters violently.

Contradiction: Two of his three wives were born outside of this country. Ivana Marie Zelnickova Trump was born in the Czech Republic and Melania (Melanija Knavs) Trump was born in Slovenia.

This is classic Limbo. A month prior, he said, "We have companies pouring in. The problem is we need workers."

How can workers be needed and immigration be discouraged? How does he get a pass when importing wives to the United States? President Thug is both people pleaser and alienator. When he lacks knowledge, he will aim at the middle or the absurd, so as not to risk the embarrassment of unfinished homework. This is most noticeable when he tells a lie or is unsure of his words. Before telling a lie, President Thug purses his lips, shifts his eyes, and then quickly inhales and grits his teeth. With arms crossed in pouty, pre-teen expression, he raises his voice and questions the questioner. Limbo deflection is his defensive shield of protection.

Limbo attitudes aren't definitive. President Thug claims to have no knowledge of the conspiracy concept of QAnon, but ironically he stated, "I don't know much about the movement other than I understand that they like me very much, which I appreciate."

A reporter told Trump that QAnon supporters believe he is "secretly saving the world from a satanic cult of pedophiles and cannibals." The president replied: "I haven't heard that. But is that supposed to be a bad thing or good thing? If I can help save the world from problems, I'm willing to do it. I'm willing to put myself out there" (Caitlin Oprysko, Politico).

President Thug is *premiocre*. An Amanda Mull article, "It's All So … Premiocre" in The Atlantic, mentions the coining of the term by writer, Venkatesh Rao. *Premiocre* (premium mediocre) is the least expensive way to gain temporary entry to a particular consumer class. Limbo is big brother to premiocre, straddling the cheap and expensive, balancing low price with extravagant perception — big, yet hollow. Trump's steaks, ties, universities, casinos, hotels, and words are all symbols of his premiocrity. He wants to be premium, but he's below mediocre.

Like a child searching for meaning and validation through deceit, Thug uses Limbo to misdirect conversations. Limbo is a state of confusion and unsettled decisions. If you advocate law and order, why would you ignore and defy subpoenas? If you believe in law and order, why cheat on taxes. The habitat in Limbo is animated suspension and arrested development. It is a twilight zone of Id, Ego, and Super ego. But President Thug defies the moral conscience of the Super Ego; he seeks the impulse of Freud's Id, which he'll crave in the Second Circle of Hell — Lust.

3

LUST - I THRICE PAID FOR SEX
CIRCLE OF HELL 2

T he Second Circle of Hell is Lust - the land of the carnal. Rippling in this realm are the imagination of all perverted, unauthorized, unsolicited, and non-consenting sexual acts. There is no way to insatiate the physical desires, infinite winds of venereal indiscretion, and hot blooded sins of unbridled eroticism. The Id of President Thug manifests itself in Lust.

Earlier in life, President Thug branded himself as a wealthy man who spent his time Caligula-style, inviting danger and behaving irresponsibly in diverse, casual sexual relationships. He unapologetically views the exploitation of women as sport. But the Access Hollywood hot mic discussions were the clear embodiment of a sexual predator, who objectifies women at all costs. His explicit comments to Billy Bush about Arianne Zucker codified his cherishing of the Second Circle.

"I better use some Tic Tacs just in case I start kissing her. You know I'm automatically attracted to beautiful [women]— I just start kissing them. It's like a magnet. Just kiss. I don't even wait. And when you're a star they let you do it. You can do anything. Grab them by the p****! You can do anything. Oh it looks good. Ooh, nice legs, huh?"

— Donald Trump caught on hot lavalier mic

President Thug also bragged about failing to seduce Nancy O'Dell.

"I moved on her, and I failed. I'll admit it. I did try and f*** her. She was married. And I moved on her very heavily. In fact, I took her out furniture shopping. She wanted to get some furniture. I said, 'I'll show you where they have some nice furniture.' I took her out furniture— [shopping], I moved on her like a b****. But I couldn't get there. And she was married. Then all of a sudden I see her, she's now got the big phony t*** and everything. She's totally changed her look."

— Donald Trump caught on hot lavalier mic

Imagine if you will, a world where President Barack Obama said the same things that President Thug murmured. If Obama made any of the earlier statements, he would have never become President of the United States. In the short run, the powerfully wicked with status get a pass, a mulligan, a do-over, while those unconnected with color in caste and class systems would have been thrown out with the trash and labeled forever. President Thug can say, "I tried to f*** her." But President Obama couldn't even utter allegiance to Rev. Jeremiah Wright.

Sex work has its place. Some professional sex work is legal and taxable in a few places around the globe. Those in the profession aren't to be judged, but to exercise caution in unpleasant situations that could occur if violent, manipulative clients take advantage of transactions, by physically harming a worker or by denying payment. Thug doesn't regard or respect boundaries and treats sex like a common commodity.

President Thug wants to be wanted so he pays others to satisfy his fanciful inclinations. While wearing silky, black pajamas, Thug awaited a knock at the door from Stormy Daniels (aka Stephanie Clifford, née Stephanie Gregory), an adult actress, entertainer, and film director. She arrives and Trump is excited. Daniels states that for Donald Trump to be so wealthy, she was surprised that he used Pert Plus shampoo and Old Spice after shave (whistle). The transaction begins, and although Trump is a germaphobe - no condom.

Daniels said, "I laid there and prayed for death."

During a rendezvous, while watching "Shark Week" with Stormy Daniels, Hillary Clinton calls Thug's phone. An awkward moment indeed, in Circle Two.

Stormy Daniels told the world this story of having an affair with Donald Trump in July of 2006 after the American Century Celebrity Golf Championship in Lake Tahoe, California. Melania had just given birth 4 months prior to the golf outing. Although non-disclosure agreements were issued, Daniels professes an ongoing affair with Trump, with multiple trysts after Lake Tahoe. NDAs don't cover everything. Before the 2016 election, Donald Trump's lawyer paid Daniels $130,000 to keep her relationship with Trump a secret.

While boarding a plane, Trump was asked by a reporter, "Did you know about the $130,000 payment made to Stormy Daniels?"

Trump hesitantly replied, "No. No, what else?"

"Then why did Michael Cohen make it [the payment] if there was no truth to the allegations?" asked the reporter.

Trump says, "Well you'll have to ask Michael Cohen. Michael is my attorney. And you'll have to ask Michael."

The reporter corners him, "Do you know where he got the money?"

"No, I don't know, no." said Trump.

President Thug has been roadkill from previous lustful activities, but he doesn't care. If lust exposes embarrassment, he shows little concern. But if lust costs him money, he pivots to rage, never apologizing for the action or offense. President Thug lives in a pre-adolescent world of playful, yet destructive ignorance. "It's just locker room banter," he defends. But boasting on his sexual exploits borders on insecurity and inadequacy. His simulated swagger is pubescent at best; longing for acceptance, cheers, envy, or congratulatory high fives from other shrinking males who have dubious thoughts of their own. President Thug is a grown man locked in raging, juvenile hormones.

How does he obtain forgiveness by his base for the projection of sins? Beth Daley, editor and general manager of The Conversation, says that "a leader like

Trump offers an opportunity to combine transgressive pleasure with the moral high ground."

His dreadful behavior is eclipsed by his shadow of power, lurking pervasively, daring to be crossed by anyone. Dozens of woman have accused President Thug of assault, rape, misappropriate touching, and lewd communication. But nothing sticks. Circle Two is his zone. He even endorsed Roy Moore, a candidate for senate, who had been alleged to have sexually abused teenage girls.

As long as powerfully corrupt men shape narratives, write history, and define laws, we may be waiting quite some time to see justice prevail when women voice the oppressive behaviors of abusive men. We saw the privilege of violent male sexual predation with Brock Turner, the former Stanford student who sexually assaulted Chanel Miller while she was unconscious. Turner was convicted of assaulting the young woman near a trash bin after they drank heavily at a fraternity party. Turner served three months, and if he wasn't considered a "golden boy" before the heinous crime, he would have been sentenced to at least 14 years in federal prison. Judge Aaron Persky said a tougher sentence "would have had a severe impact on him" — and he did not think Turner was dangerous. Turner's aggravating crime and punishment was met with the mitigating factor of him being a first-time offender, a promising student, and a recruited swimmer with championship potential. Chanel Miller was violated and given no honor. She wrote the book, *Know My Name: A Memoir*, just to restore her respect and dignity. The judge was eventually recalled and Brock Turner carries the sex offender label.

Sexism is real. Brock Turner and Aaron Persky are examples of men who believe women are expendable, disposable, and worthless. They share the reptilian habitat of President Thug.

Lust is selfish, having no care for the victim. It only seeks it's goal - pleasure by any means necessary.

Here is a short list of alleged lustful, violent, and intimidating acts for which President Thug has been accused:

- Rachel Crooks accused Thug of inappropriately kissing her and not letting her go.
- Jill Harth accused Thug of sexual assault, harassment, and groping.
- Stormy Daniels won back her legal fees and court costs totaling $44,100 from

Trump, but Thug still denies paying her $130,000 in hush money.

- Ninni Laaksonen alleged that Trump groped her from behind.
- Jessica Drake said that Trump had inappropriate, unwanted sexual contact with her at a golf tournament. Drake refused his advances and Trump asked her, "What do you want? How much?"
- Cassandra Searles alleged sexual misconduct. She said, "One guy [Trump] treated us like cattle [having] us line up so he could get a closer look at his property."
- Karen Virginia accused Trump of grabbing her by the arm, and touching her breast. She later made the statement to Trump, "Your random moment of sexual pleasure came at my expense and affected me greatly."
- Summer Zervos, contestant on *The Apprentice*, accused Trump of sexual assault, "thrusting his genitals."
- Cathy Heller accused Donald Trump of sexual misconduct at a Mother's Day brunch at Mar-a-Lago.
- Samantha Holvey said at pageants,

"[Trump] would look you over from head to toe like we were just meat...sexual objects, ... not people."

- Tasha Dixon was disgusted by his disregard for women. She alleged sexual misconduct when Trump would appear in dressing rooms of pageants. During a Howard Stern interview, Trump admitted, "I'll go backstage before a show and everyone's getting dressed and ready and everything else. And you know, no men are anywhere. And I'm allowed to go in because I'm the owner of the pageant. And therefore, I'm inspecting it. I want to make sure everything is good. Is everyone okay? You know they're standing there with no clothes. And you see these incredible looking women. And so I sort of get away with things like that."

- When asked had he ever had sex with Miss Universe or Miss USA contestants, he said, "I never comment on things like that." The interviewer asks, "Give us the first letter of the country [for the ladies] you had sex with." Trump replied, "How many letters are there?"

- When asked had he ever dated a Playboy Playmate, he said, " I refuse to answer that question…it may be true." He says this right in front of Melania.
- Mariah Billado, a former Miss Teen USA contestant, claimed Trump behaved inappropriately during the pageant, appearing unannounced to look at the teenaged girls.
- Jessica Leeds alleged unwanted sexual advances, with Trump touching her on the breasts and under her skirt. She described him as an "octopus."
- Mindy McGillivray accused Donald Trump of groping her at a concert at Mar-a-Lago.
- Jennifer Murphy said he kissed her without consent.
- Natasha Stoynoff said Trump pinned her to a wall and kissed her. "I remember his weight. "He leans on you like an oversexed mastodon." After denying he had ever met her, Trump said, "Look at her… I don't think so."
- Lisa Boyne alleged that Trump and John C. looked under women's skirts at an

event to see if the women were wearing underwear.

- Kristin Anderson said Trump reached under her skirt and touched her without consent.
- Temple Taggart claimed Donald Trump sexually harassed her, by grabbing her and kissing her on the lips at a Miss USA pageant rehearsal. He claims to have never met her, although when convenient, he remembers meeting her with her parents.
- Trump was friends with Jeffrey Epstein and as he condemns Epstein's behavior, he also incriminates himself. "It is even said that he [Epstein] likes beautiful women as much as I do, and many of them are on the younger side." The awkward sentence structure places just as much blame on Trump as it does Epstein.

President Thug's journey through the Second Circle has been a long and pleasurable one. He wallows and basks in the throws of sport-like infidelity and indecency, sleazy and unbecoming, indeed. Next stop, Circle Three: Gluttony.

4

GLUTTONY - I'M NEVER SATISFIED
CIRCLE OF HELL 3

President Thug is gluttonous to a fault. He craves everything he sees: the valuable, the mediocre, and the worthless. Attention, money, status, and power are the tenets of this man's obsession with acquisition. His insatiable appetite is repulsive, but those closest to him give no warning of indigestion. He just consumes, vomits, spends and eats, again and again. His philosophy is an overindulgent one, having no redemption other than repeating the act of engorging.

In the Third Circle, the tormented must swim in hot sewage. Trying to escape is futile. The guardian of gluttony is Cerberus, the three-headed dog, positioned to bite and claw at those who devoured plenty, but desired more. His ferocious barks and ravenous behavior are a reminder of coveted excess. Overzealous sensation for control, earthly providence, and hoarding are natural to gluttony. President Thug is also a glutton for punishment. It matters little to him that trouble or consequence could be imminent. He would rather harm others, take the credit and be noticed, than to help others and blend into obscurity.

The law of diminishing returns is meaningless to President Thug. He will attach value to anything he deems worthy, but his tax returns are southern exposure, creating a sunny, open book to his frailty. But boasting about his possessions gives him temporary solace. He contradicts himself often by demanding money and power, but distances himself to debt and pay out. His verbal play is demonstrated when looking for a witch who's cooking curses in the cauldron, not realizing he is the witch he's seeking. "This is a continuation of the witch hunt, the greatest witch hunt in history. There's never been anything like it," Thug shouted.

Foreign governments have rented space in Thug owned buildings. His gluttony didn't see that this may have been against the law. Arrogant and gauche, President Thug and his lawyers argued that they weren't aware that "paying your hotel bill was an emolument." Private financial interests can compromise leaders of governments. President Thug never put his companies in a blind trust, nor did he divest from his companies while holding office. The United States taxpayers have paid over $1 million for over 2,000 nightly room rentals at Trump's hotels and clubs. Not only did President Thug hold office — he also steered contracts to his properties. Staffers, family members, Secret Service, and Trump's family have been billing the United States government (David Fahrenthold, Washington Post).

The gluttony continues with the maneuvering of hotel and entertainment contracts to the Trump Organization.

- At least nine foreign governments were involved in hosting events at a Trump property: Afghanistan, Cyprus, Ireland, Japan, Philippines, Kuwait, United Arab Emirates, Saudi Arabia and Turkey.
- At least nine foreign governments rented or purchased property in buildings or communities owned by Trump businesses: Kuwait, Iraq, Saudi Arabia, China, Malaysia, Slovakia, Thailand, India and the European Union.
- Representatives of at least five foreign

governments — Georgia, Nigeria, Malaysia, Romania and Saudi Arabia — have stayed at a Trump property.

- Foreign governments have improved infrastructure in a way that benefited Trump properties in Indonesia and Panama.
- At least eight foreign governments or their representatives attended parties or gatherings at Trump properties: Brazil, Dominica, Georgia, Nigeria, Russia, Turkey, Malaysia and Qatar (NBC News).

Hunger doesn't have to lead to gluttony. But not to be outdone, President Thug wanted to buy Greenland. He said it would be, "Strategically… interesting."

Denmark's prime minister Mette Frederiksen quickly reminded Thug that "Greenland is not for sale."

When your tummy is full and you want more, a responsible adult must tell you, "No." Because Thug couldn't have what he desired, he became embarrassed and canceled his trip to Greenland. What's worse than a spoiled brat? A spoiled thug who thought he could buy Greenland.

5

GREED - I WANT WHAT I WANT
CIRCLE OF HELL 4

G reedy - Miserly - Avaricious - Hoarders ——
In the Fourth Circle, souls who are stingy
and the prodigal have to push rocks to the center and
to the periphery of a vast circular area. They are
divided into two groups – those who hoarded money
and possessions and those who carelessly and extrav-
agantly spent it. The pushing of heavy boulders with
their chests symbolizes selfishness and disregard for
others while seeking fortune during their lifetime.
Dante and Virgil don't speak to them and President
Thug is confused by the monotony and anguish of
souls being punished for hoarding and spending. They
see pastors, priests, and popes who spiritually and
financially abused their churches, pop stars who
flaunted their wealth, and misers who kept all of their

riches from those who needed it most. In this realm are the reckless, wasteful, boisterously arrogant spenders and misers with insatiable greed, who are doomed to push rocks against one another -- forever.

In the Electronic Arts video game version of Dante's Inferno, the character Hoarder/Waster is a menacing depiction of two characters sewn together, symbolizing an extreme clenching of possessions and the squandering of others. One wants to collect and hoard wealth while the other wants to spend wealth. Money freely drips in and out of Hoarder/Waster. The characters' torment and tempt victims with the lure of gold.

President Thug is a Hoarder/Waster. Instead of visiting other properties that may be more convenient to himself and staff, President Thug spends time and money at his own resorts, billing the expenses to the Federal Government - LHT (Low Hanging Theft). Thirty-seven political functions added $3.8 million to the Trump coffers. Hoarder/Wasters will find, hide, spend, and parade money with no tact or social graces. Thug proposed cutting $8.6 billion from the housing budget, but allowed HUD Secretary Ben Carson to spend $31,000 on a dining set for his office and another $165,000 on lounge furniture. Housing development for lower income families was not a priority for Trump and Carson. But buying a lavish dining set was mandatory for the Hoarder/Wasters.

In classic Hoarder/Waster fashion, President Thug had several of his companies apply for $21 million in SBA Loans earmarked for businesses suffering during the Covid-19 crisis. Unapologetically, the Thug family pocketed the funds with no punishment, no apology, and no political remorse. Jared Kushner and Donald Trump, Jr., led the Thug brigade by cutting the line, collecting funds in front of 30 million small businesses more worthy of the funding. This is hoarding on a high level because if the Thug businesses claimed to have billionaire status and accounts, why would they apply for SBA loans? Tricky.

Thug's son, Eric Trump, needed a shut-off valve on his braggadocio of the Thug Empire. He talked so much about being funded by foreign bankers that subpoenas and suspicions stacked. President Thug has a knack for inflating assets when he wants to appear wealthy or if he needs loans, but downplays his worth when tax time rolls around. Thug runs to microphones if he has something to sell, but hides from microscopes if he has secret business dealings.

Always seeking an edge and tempting emoluments issues, Ivanka Trump promoted a $10,000 necklace on a *60 Minutes* episode. Kellyanne Conway broke the rules by promoting Ivanka Trump's retail brand during a newscast. In an unadulterated motive, she said "Go buy Ivanka's stuff is what I would tell you...I'm going to give a free commercial here. Go buy it today, everybody." Melania Trump has also hawked jewelry during the administration as well. They mocked the American public and have been a disgrace to sacred leadership positions of government. Thugs cannot be trusted.

President Thug refused to divest from his real estate companies or to place his assets in a blind trust, as encouraged by the U.S. Office of Government Ethics. Thug chose to entrust business operations of his companies to his sons, Eric Trump and Donald Trump, Jr. According to the Director of the U.S. Office of Government Ethics, Trump's arrangement "doesn't meet the standards that the best of his nominees are meeting and that every President in the past four decades has met." Hunted by impropriety, the emoluments clause forbids government officials from accepting "any present, Emolument, Office, or Title, of any kind whatever, from any King, Prince, or foreign State."

Greed abounds and as a discourtesy to would-be members, President Thug doubled the Mar-a-Lago initiation fees. In another premiocre move, he placed a bet on his presidential status by boosting fees from $100,000 to $200,000.

Sins of a so-called billionaire:

- The New York Times reported that he only paid $750 on his Federal Income taxes (Buettner, McIntire, Craig, Collins). He claimed double the loss on businesses than capital gains. Trump says this about not paying taxes, "That makes me smart."
- He claimed $100 million in losses on his leaked 2005 tax return, paying $38 million instead of $76 million.
- The incarnation of avarice is Melania Trump preferring to live away from the White House, costing $26.8 million per year for added security. If they are so rich, why couldn't the Thug family pay for its own security?
- Let them eat cake. The Thug administration suggested canceling food assistance to 40 million Americans.
- Months after a series of meetings held in the White House between Jared Kushner and the CEO of Apollo Global Management, a massive wealth

management fund, Apollo, lent Kushner Companies $184 million dollars to refinance their mortgage on a Chicago skyscraper. Earlier, Kushner's firm received an even larger loan of $325 million from Citigroup after Kushner met the CEO of Citigroup at the White House.

- Cheapest of Skates - Trump was not interested in paying livable wages. He would much rather pay as little as possible, so he chose to hire undocumented workers at Trump National Golf Club in Bedminster, N.J., while telling the rest of the world not to hire undocumented workers (Fahrentold and Partlow, Washington Post).

- He is a walking sham, a man determined to take care of himself at everyone else's peril. He is the greediest of the greedy. Immigrants did everything at Thug's complexes, yet he refers to immigration as a tragedy, a national crisis, and a scheme to hurt "American workers." President Thug says illegal immigration hurts taxpayers and it compromises public safety. But he has no problem hiring undocumented workers when it's time to pinch pennies. He is Ebenezer Scrooge on steroids. He is a maniac without a compass, without a conscience, and without recalibration. He doesn't mind pushing boulders in the Fourth Circle, because he is still king of all Hoarder/Wasters. He lives for Avarice.

6

WRATH - MY ANGER IS UNCONTROLLABLE

CIRCLE OF HELL 5

Wrath is President Thug's oxygen. His anger brings a sullen mood of negative energy. He is the human manifestation of a bad attitude, so the Fifth Circle suits him just fine. In this level of Hell, we see the victims tormented on the banks of the River Styx. President Thug is perfect for wrath. He says," I bring out rage in people."

In Wrath, there is constant fighting in swamps. Wrath is one of the hot blooded sins. Humans drown in their own anger here. Souls cry out in fear.

Demons give clearance for Dante and Virgil to proceed to the lower gates of hell. President Thug joins them and remarks that this circle isn't that scary. His demeanor is intimidating. President Thug is angry, even when he appears to be happy.

"The findings show how Trump uses an informal, direct, and provoking communication style to construct and reinforce the concept of a homogeneous people and a homeland threatened by the dangerous other. Moreover, Trump employs positive self-presentation and negative other-presentation to further his agenda via social media. This study demonstrates how his top-down use of Twitter may lead to the normalization of right-wing populist discourses, and thus aims to contribute to the understanding of right-wing populist discourse online" (Ramona Kreis, Journal of Language and Politics).

President Thug shows his fangs in Circle 5. Because he has no filter or conscience, the loss of human life is just collateral coincidental damage for which he takes no credit. Thug ordered a raid in Yemen that collected no intelligence on enemies. One Navy SEAL, five U.S. soldiers, and 30 civilians were killed, including children. President Thug vaguely and insincerely expressed his sentiments to the loss of life. Thug's coldness only compares to Hitler, and his bunkers may be nearing.

Throughout his wicked life, Thug has shown anger, eventually leading to violence, fraud, and betrayal. But for now, racism and anger make for a devilish mix. Thug loathes Black people and he has low expectations and trust for them. His anger is rooted in stereotypes from a bygone age. He is trapped in an era before the civil rights movement.

> Trump once said, "Black guys counting my money! I hate it. The only kind of people I want counting my money are short guys that wear yarmulkes every day. It's not Black people's fault, because laziness is a trait in Blacks. It really is, I believe that. It's not anything they can control."

Nobody glorifies and enjoys firing employees. This is President Thug's specialty, and he honed his skills for firing on his NBC show, *The Apprentice*. The practice continued with Sally Yates, Preet Bharara, Mark Esper, Chris Krebs, and James Comey who were all fired by President Thug. He doesn't fire you face-to-face. He is a coward who tweets the firing or instructs his minions to do the dirty work. When terminating Comey, President Thug deliberately fired him while he was at a speaking engagement on leadership to his FBI team in California. Comey found out on CNN, and to add injury, President Thug wanted Comey to get his own transportation back to his home. Ugly.

If any woman ever supports President Thug, she

should seriously rethink her love affair with Stockholm Syndrome. Planned Parenthood provides the following services for women and President Thug's right-hand man (Vice President Pence) decided to vote for a bill that would defund women's services and advocacy from Planned Parenthood. Pence voted against Planned Parenthood's ability to provide the following: COVID-19 information, birth control, cancer awareness and screening, emergency contraception, health and wellness, pregnancy information, sex education, sexual dysfunction information, abortion, sexual orientation information, gender identity information, narrative explanation of relationships, information on consent and sexual assault, and detailed information on sexually transmitted diseases. President Thug and Pence were notorious in trying to unravel Title IX and Title X laws. Title IX is a federal civil rights law passed as part of the Education Amendments of 1972. This law protects people from discrimination based on sex in education programs or activities that receive Federal financial assistance. Title X was legally designed to prioritize the needs of low-income families or uninsured people (including those who are not eligible for Medicaid) who might not otherwise have access to these health care services. These services are provided at reduced or no cost. President Thug's anger and volition had specific targets, many of which were repeals of Obama-era laws.

President Barack Obama never ordered to have President Thug's voice recorded by phone or any other recording conduit or device. Thug has made several attempts to make President Obama his enemy. He lacked evidence that Obama illegally tapped Trump Tower during the 2016 election. Thug responded to the reporter, "I have my own opinions. You can have your own opinions. OK, it's enough. Thank you." He then stormed out of the interview.

President Thug feels threatened when he cannot answer a question, when he's wrong, or when he is embarrassed. During an exchange with a reporter, Thug broke the protocol of being polite and presidential. Kevin Freking and Jonathan Lemire from the Associated Press, journal the exchange between President Trump and Reuters journalist Jeff Mason.

"Are you talking to me?," said President Thug.

Jaw thrust forward and ready to rumble, President Donald Trump plowed his way through a day of questions about his controversial phone call with Ukraine's leader, his private anger about the House impeachment effort bursting into full public view.

"Did you hear me? Did you hear me? Ask him a

question," the president, pointing to his counterpart from Finland.

The president was intimidated and embarrassed because he was impeached and journalists insisted for him to answer a question. Trump said he did nothing wrong in what he repeatedly dubbed "a perfect call" with Ukrainian President Volodymyr Zelenskiy.

Jeff Mason pressed Trump and Thug Life came out.

"Are you talking to me?," Trump backfired.

Trump wasn't ready for Mason's inquiry.

"Did you hear me? Did you hear me? Ask him a question," Trump ordered, pointing to Niinisto.

Minutes later, the news conference ended and Trump stalked off the stage, again alone (Freking and Lemire, AP).

President Thug is not a smart man. He is governed by feelings, passions, shortcuts, and wrath. A spoiled, silver spoon lifestyle with little background knowledge, a wealth of mean spiritedness, and limited literacy skills will always lead to a fight — especially if those smarter than Thug have the upper hand. He was a tempestuous and petulant president with bellicose tendencies. There's much more to come in the Sixth Circle.

7

HERESY - I AM YOUR MESSIAH
CIRCLE OF HELL 6

H eresy is a religious belief that runs contrary to orthodox religious Christian doctrine, will-fully and persistently rejecting any article of faith. Heretics will be buried in burning stone graves forever. Some of the heretics will make attempts to escape the fiery tombs, but heavy stones prevent them from moving. Farinata degli Uberti, the Florentine leader of the Ghibelline faction, rises to say hello to Dante, Virgil, and Trump. Having never opened a history book, Trump asks, "Who is this Farinata guy?"

President Thug is the Exorcist II: The Heretic. He is both Dismisser and Perverter of Religion, confusing denominations, persuasions, sects, and practices. The editor of a major Christian magazine, had to come to Jesus by telling his readers that Trump is no good for the faith and the country.

> "He has hired and fired a number of people who are now convicted criminals. He himself has admitted to immoral actions in business and his relationship with women, about which he remains proud. His Twitter feed alone—with its habitual string of mischaracterizations, lies, and slanders—is a near perfect example of a human being who is morally lost and confused."
>
> Mark Galli, Christianity Today

Writer, Peter Wehner stated,

> "Mr. Trump is a toxic figure in American politics. If you want to know how toxic he is, he has a 70 percent unfavorable rating. Mr. Trump is toxic for a reason. He is nativist, xenophobic, cruel, vindictive, emotionally unstable, narcissistic, obsessive, and yet, he is without an economic agenda or a governing philosophy. He's stunningly ignorant on issues, and he seems to be a person who's given over to profanity and demagogy."

Wehner also mentions other unethical Trump behavior such as:

1. authorizing hush-money payments to a porn star,
2. misogyny,
3. predatory sexual behavior,
4. sexualization of his daughters, and
5. his use of tabloids to humiliate his first wife, Ivana, when he was having an affair with Marla Maples.

While campaigning, President Thug showed the so-called Liberty University evangelicals and students that he wasn't up to the task of believing in Christ, following Christian principles, or reciting simple Bible verses. While professing that he was going to protect Christianity, he butchered the reciting of Second Corinthians, and the laughter from the audience made him a bit uneasy. Trump says,

Now the Lord is the Spirit, and where the Spirit of the Lord is, there is freedom. Two Corinthians, right, Two Corinthians 3:17. That's the whole ballgame. [Laughter from audience] Where the Spirit of the Lord,... right? [Laughter from audience] Where the Spirit of the Lord is, there is liberty, and here there is Liberty College, but Liberty University, but it is so true."

He uses evangelicals as trinkets and souvenirs of Christian patronage, amplifying his roguish disregard for religious reverence. He says, "I'm a protestant, very proud of it. Presbyterian to be exact," but has no idea what Presbyterian beliefs entail. He is the heretics' heretic. Baseless.

McKay Coppins, writer for The Atlantic, has illuminated Trump's dark dismissal of orthodoxy and belief. He mocks the prayers of others, and claims that God is on his side. On a few occasions, Thug refused to recite the Apostles' Creed. The Apostles' Creed is a statement of Christian belief commonly recited during services in a number of Christian denominations.

Carefully and critically think through this contradiction. He claims to be a believer and advocate of the evangelical movement, but couldn't force his lips to recite these words:

"I believe in God, the Father Almighty, Creator of Heaven and earth; and in Jesus Christ, His only Son Our Lord, Who was conceived by the Holy

Spirit, born of the Virgin Mary, suffered under Pontius Pilate, was crucified, died, and was buried. He descended into Hell; the third day He rose again from the dead; He ascended into Heaven, and sitteth at the right hand of God, the Father almighty; from thence He shall come to judge the living and the dead. I believe in the Holy Spirit, the holy Catholic Church, the communion of saints, the forgiveness of sins, the resurrection of the body and life everlasting. Amen."

Journalist, John Ward wrote,

"Striking that all the former Presidents and First Ladies recited the Apostles' Creed, but Trump and Melania stood silently and did not. The creeds are at the heart of historic orthodox Christianity."

Trump is on record having said that preachers are "full of s***. They're all hustlers. Man, [Christianity] that's some racket."

President Thug only honors evangelicals when they can deliver a vote. Other than that, he hates the very premise of religious sentiment. In Michael Cohen's book *Disloyal,* Cohen remembers what

Trump said after evangelicals prayed for him. President Thug said, "Can you believe that bullshit?"

The religious right has bought into Thug's shapeshifting. They excuse him in exchange for Roe v. Wade, fundraising, and the restoration of a perverted sense that America was once a great country.

Heresy was on full display when Rev. John Jenkins, President of Notre Dame, discussed a plan to open the university regardless of science guidelines. He opened the campus with no regard for safety, but with deep devotion to tuition dollars. While Notre Dame was logging new Coronavirus cases, they insisted on opening the campus. President Thug has a way of influencing and bullying leaders to do what he says regardless of responsibility. Rev. Jenkins was later diagnosed with a positive Covid-19 outcome, after attending the White House for a super-spreading Supreme Court nominee gathering for Amy Coney Barrett.

Notre Dame professors expressed concern about contact tracing, irresponsible coronavirus-spreading behavior, and traveling.

"I'm afraid for every single person on campus, every staff member, every administrator, every student, every faculty member."

Notre Dame faculty member

Another professor said,

"I think it's important to remember, the biggest single decision was made unilaterally by John Jenkins back in May."

Notre Dame Professor Richard Williams

Cults have parasites and hosts. But the head of a cult is more parasitic than the members. The charismatic individual brainwashes members into providing unconditional love, money, loyalty, and honor to the leader. But the members don't realize that they are the hosts the parasite relies on for sustenance, riches, and power. A cult is a system of religious veneration and devotion directed toward a particular figure or object. Cult leaders need members and cult members need meaning. Therefore, the cult members clothe themselves in the spirit of the charismatic leader and the organization. This is MAGA — a cult built into a major American political party.

President Thug chose not to take credit for his Jim Jones, David Koresh, and Marshall Applewhite motives, but his suggestion to the cult was to ingest and inject disinfectants and beams of light to fight coronavirus. This became the not-so-mild equivalent to Kool-Aid, cyanide, sedatives, vodka, sleeping pills, and grape juice. Thug took no blame or credit for suggesting the actions, though making it clear during a White House briefing. The American Association of Poison Control Centers reported 3,401 cases of disinfectant poisoning in March 2020 and 3,609 cases in April, after President Thug's suggestions. The numbers for 2019 were 1,756 and 1,628, respectively. Bleach cases in March and April of 2020 were 5,068 and 5,739, respectively. Bleach poisonings the year prior were 3,184 and 3,242, respectively. President Thug's words may have correlated with an increased number of poisoning incidents.

Heretics having no moral GPS can put cult members in serious danger. President Thug called churches "essential places," ordering governors to open them in a pandemic. The proposal here is to convince the masses to obey God, to defy knowledge, and to risk dying. This unprocessed, immature impulse was as convincing as a QAnon plot. By the way, QAnon is listed as a possible domestic terror threat and QAnon supporters don't even know the identity of Q. Now that's cultic.

Bible belt Trump voters, MAGA, and the Trump cult, all point to the hypocrisy of the evangelical swarm. President Thug used Bibles for props, and used those who profess the Bible as property, able to be manipulated at the drop of a tweet. Burning in tombs for an eternity is permanent residence in Circle Six. Holding a Bible in front of a church after tear gassing protesters will not get Thug out of the fire. He did this to stage a phony photo opportunity. Heresy.

President Thug believes that his religion is no religion, and the cult sees the nihilist as the messiah.

8

VIOLENCE - I DON'T CARE IF I
HURT YOU

CIRCLE OF HELL 7

Violence – The Seventh Circle of Hell. This is the realm of murderers, warmongers, psychopaths, self-harmers, exorbitant usurers, tyrants, and blasphemers. The tormented swim in boiling streams of blood bordered by beaches of flaming sands. Dante, Virgil, and President Thug see Chiron and thousands of centaurs shooting the murderous souls trying to escape the bubbling river. Thug is nervous because he knows that his actions and words have led to people dying. He has also harmed himself and has committed crimes against nature.

To unjustly kill someone deserves harsh punishment. In this realm, terror is constant with the wing-flapping intimidation of the Harpies. Trees filled with violent souls are ripped, scraped, and eaten by the

Harpies. They are human-like creatures with owl-shaped bodies and faces with beaks. Sharp claws, ominous wings, and female breasts complete this mythological monster. Ravenous Harpies riddle the Sixth Circle.

President Thug acted as a Harpy and had no remorse or conscience when he separated families. Thousands of small children and infants were ripped from their mother's arms and denied to see them. Under President Thug, the United States placed children in cage camps and were denied toothpaste, soap, privacy, parental visits, human rights, and dignity. This is violent and would have been seen as unimaginable and unacceptable if the people weren't poor and Mexican. The outrage was toned down because Thug supporters have no empathy for humans from a different experience. Adam Serwer of The Atlantic states that, "The Trump administration's commitment to deterring immigration through cruelty has made horrifying conditions in detention facilities inevitable."

The Trump administration has deliberately inflicted suffering on children to deter illegal immigration, with its use of family separation. It has altered immigration policy and the asylum process so as to force the authorities to hold migrants, whether they have properly sought asylum at a port of entry or crossed illegally, and has made it more difficult for children to be released to sponsors in the United States by threatening to arrest and deport family members who lack legal status. In private, some Border Patrol agents consider migrant deaths a laughing matter; others are succumbing to depression, anxiety, or substance abuse (Serwer, The Atlantic).

Dismissing a person's credentials without proof is a violent act. President Thug claimed that President Obama never attended an Ivy League school, "[This] president came out of nowhere. Came out of nowhere. In fact, I'll go a step further: The people that went to school with him, they never saw him, they don't know who he is. It's crazy."

President Obama attended Occidental College for two years, then transferred to Columbia to finish undergrad. He then attended Harvard Law and became the first Black person to edit the Harvard Law Review. President Thug hates President Obama on a primal level. With his hatred and disgust for Black people, he can't figure out how a Black person could achieve so much and have such a high approval rating while in office. It baffles him, so he defaults to the creation of curious conspiracies and dubious rumors.

President Thug snarled and hissed during an interview with Fox News. "He [Obama] doesn't have a birth certificate, or if he does, there's something on that certificate that is very bad for him."

On another occasion, President Thug babbles incoherently. "There are three things that could happen. And one of them did happen. He was perhaps born in Kenya. Very simple, OK? He was perhaps born in this country. But, said he was born in Kenya because if you say you were born in Kenya, you got aid and you got into colleges. People were doing that. So perhaps he was born in this country, and that has a very big chance. Or, you know, who knows?" said Thug.

Birtherism is a movement in the United States of America that doubts that Barack Obama is a natural-born U.S. citizen, implying his ineligibility to be President. Birtherism is violent because the belief can trigger radicalized conspiracy cults to act on false pretense, hurting an individual's reputation, livelihood, freedom, and family safety. Thug continues the lies of birtherism, aiming his hatred at the Obamas. The thoughts and actions that secure your damnation in the Sixth Circle are violent, and Thug doubles down on birtherism.

"If you are going to be president of the United States you have to be born in this country. And there is a doubt as to whether or not he was. He doesn't have a birth certificate. He may have one, but there's something on that, maybe religion, maybe it says he is a Muslim. I don't know. Maybe he doesn't want that. Or he may not have one. But I will tell you this. If he wasn't born in this country, it's one of the great scams of all time," screamed Thug.

With such gibberish, how did the American polity allow Thug to say and do whatever came to his mind, regardless of mistruth, malcontent, and malice?

Michelle Obama claimed that President Thug had put her family in danger. The former first lady said she would "never forgive" Donald Trump for promoting the false birther conspiracy stories. Michelle Obama reportedly called the conspiracy "crazy and mean-spirited" and said it endangered her family. "What if someone with an unstable mind loaded a gun and drove to Washington? What if that person went looking for our girls? Donald Trump, with his loud and reckless innuendos, was putting my family's safety at risk."

In response to the "birther" conspiracy theory, the State of Hawaii released Barack Obama's birth certificate.

Spouting and planting untruths like a 6th grade boy in a cafeteria, Thug insults and lies to cover his ineptitude and insecurity. He's mean, nasty, and vindictive. Trump hates BLACK LIVES MATTER; he hates women's movements; he hates Democrats; he hates successful business people, he hates billionaires who have more wealth; he hates everything that doesn't fit his narrative. He believes hate symbols are just emojis.

He bragged about having brainwashed followers to forgive any violent act he may commit. "They say I have the most loyal people -- did you ever see that? I could stand in the middle of Fifth Avenue and shoot somebody, and I wouldn't lose any voters, OK? It's, like, incredible."

Quoting a former Miami police Chief, Walter Headley, President Thug harkened to an old, violent cliché: "Any difficulty and we will assume control but, when the looting starts, the shooting starts."

President Thug compared bad policing (shooting Jacob Blake seven times in the back) to missing a golf putt. "Just like in a golf tournament, they miss a three-foot [putt]—they choke." Golf matters more than Black lives to him.

President Thug has highlighted and glorified violence in numerous actions:

- He tweeted that coronavirus "only killed 9,000 people."

- He blamed the California fires on a lack of sweeping up leaves. "I said, you gotta clean your floors, you gotta clean your forests — there are many, many years of leaves and broken trees and they're like, like, so flammable, you touch them and it goes up."

- While 1,500 people were dying daily to Covid-19, Thug remarked, "It will go away like things go away."

- Poisoning occurs when neurotoxic substances are in a water supply. Trump repealed the Mercury Effluent Rule regulating the proper disposal of the toxic element. Mercury can disrupt brain function and harm the nervous system. It is especially harmful to pregnant women, babies and young children, even at tiny levels of exposure (Natural Resources Defense Council).

- Trump proposed a 40% budget cut to the National Oceanic and Atmospheric Administration. He has denied hurricane direction and speeds with his own black

permanent markers, and his administration
refused to admit that climate change harms
the environment. They also changed
wording on the EPA website. "Climate and
Energy Resources for State, Local and
Tribal Governments" was rebranded as
"Energy Resources for State, Local and
Tribal Governments." Climate change
remarks were removed 15 times.

- Cutting the budget of the National
  Institutes of Health by 20% are acts of
  violence toward science and humanity.
- The Trump administration refused to
  regulate perchlorate, a toxic chemical that
  contaminates water, causing fetal and
  infant brain damage.
- The Trump administration asked the
  Supreme Court to destroy the Affordable
  Care Act, during the pandemic. President
  Thug never proposed a health care bill to
  replace The ACA.
- President Thug didn't care about workers
  who had to endure safety hazards and
  labor compromises. He signed a bill that
  blocked President Obama's Fair Pay and
  Safe Workplaces bill.

- Knowing that his rallies were Covid-19 super-spreading events, those choosing to attend Trump rallies agreed to sign waivers that prevented them from suing the campaign or President Thug if they contracted COVID-19.

- On several occasions including an Illinois rally and a Kentucky gathering, President Thug created discord by inciting violence.

- President Thug aligned himself with Andrew Jackson. In 1838 and 1839, as part of Andrew Jackson's Native American removal policy, the Cherokee nation was forced to give up land east of the Mississippi River and to migrate to an area in present-day Oklahoma. The Cherokee people called this journey the "Trail of Tears," due to the devastating effects. The migrants faced hunger, disease, and exhaustion on the forced march. Over 4,000 out of 15,000 of the Cherokees died (John Ehle, Trail of Tears).

- President Thug called for the execution of teenagers who were accused of raping a woman in Central Park. In brutal, demagogic fashion, he wrote and paid for ads that angrily stated, "BRING BACK THE DEATH PENALTY. BRING BACK OUR POLICE!" The teens were exonerated after spending several years in prison, but Thug believes to this day that they are guilty, though no DNA evidence placed any of the teens at the crime or near the victim. He has never apologized.

- Thug called reporters at CNN dumb bastards. Would any other president get away with calling the free press and television news services such a name? His quote, "They are getting tired of the pandemic, aren't they? You turn on CNN, that's all they cover. 'Covid, Covid, Pandemic, Covid, Covid.' You know why? They're trying to talk everybody out of voting. People aren't buying it, CNN, you dumb bastards."

- Thug eliminated healthcare subsidies for low income Americans.

- 400,000 U.S. citizens in Puerto Rico still lacked power in their homes and businesses for 5 months after Hurricane Maria. President Thug said, "We can't keep FEMA, the Military, and the First

Responders in P.R. forever!" He didn't realize that Puerto Rico is a territory of the United States.

- 25 endangered species lost protections due to President Thug's disregard for climate change.
- Advocating violence with no remorse, President Thug asked supporters at a rally a question about migrants. "How do you stop these people?" An audience member shouted, "Shoot them!" The president pumped back in mob style, "Only in the Panhandle!"

President Thug doesn't feel consequences because he rarely has to face them. He pays his way out, hires lawyers to defend him, or he denies the action, disparaging the person who accused him of the deviant behaviors. He is cold and distant, with no love for anyone but himself. He is violent, roguish, raging, and thuggish.

9

FRAUD - NO, YOU CAN'T SEE MY TAXES
CIRCLE OF HELL 8

President Thug's whole life is mired in deceit, so Circle 8 stands to have great relevance. He is the fraudulent falsifier, who sows discord. Geryon carries Dante, Virgil, and President Thug to see the captivity of the fraudulent, including pimps and seducers who are mercilessly whipped by demons and flatterers who are neck deep in human waste.

Selling church offices, roles, and sacred things is a trait of Simon Magus, who offered payment to two of Jesus's disciples in exchange for the power to heal. The selling of influence, position, and healing looms prevalent in the Thug Administration. These sellers of healing are placed in holes head first with their legs exposed and burned. They are the perverters of spirit, selling or buying ecclesiastical pardons, offices, and religious leaders. They charge fees for blessings, extorting money through guilt of tithing and offerings (not for God's glory and kingdom building). This fraudulent treatment of parishioners has paid for the wealth of priests, prosperity preachers, pulpit pimps, and the building of great cathedrals, mega churches, and monuments. They trick church goers into thinking salvation is a financial transaction. The threat is clear, "Give to the church or go straight to Hell."

"Nobody knows the system better than me, which is why I alone can fix it." President Thug's statements are hyperbole, but he acts with the mindset of sorcerer, diviner, magician, and fortune teller. But in the circle, he sees that this punishment is painful, with the perpetrators having contorted bodies, heads turned backward, with eyes crying blood and tears.

President Thug is a barrator, tormenting others with groundless lawsuits; he is a brangler and petti-fogger. He has misused and abused people since childhood. He is both, con man and corrupt politician, subject to the circle's pool of boiling tar. He lives among the hypocrites who pretend to hold beliefs, and whose actions are not consistent with claimed philosophies. Although beautiful on the outside, the coat of lead is heavy and hideous on the inside, wearing him down.

President Thug is a thief who dishonors businesses and contractors who have performed work for him. Not paying his fair share to the government leads him to the avenue of sniping snakes and reptiles. Columns of fire surround evil counselors and schismatic sowers of discord are split from head to groin by sword. The realm is agonizing and President Thug sees how his double-minded lifestyle has condemned family members, friends, followers, and sycophants.

President Thug is a falsifier of metal, persons, coins, and words. Falsifiers in Hell are subject to skin that itches incessantly while demons prevent scratching for relief. Falsifiers lead others astray, twisting the truth, and breaking trust on purpose. He is the leader of the panderers and seducers, walking left and right while the guilty are being whipped by flying demons. Sellers and renters of people are here. Demons with swords hack at the unapologetic. Their wounds heal but their bodies are torn apart, in repeated agony. The most demonic are beheaded and are sent to the 9th circle.

President Thug has told more than 45,000 lies over the last 25 years (an underestimate at best). The Washington Post reported that on average, Thug tells five lies per day (on record - not counting the lies with no record). It's in his nature and nurture. Given a pass by family members, due to unremarkable parenting, Thug invents stories that are fanciful, endearing to his wants and needs. He is fiction, but tries to convince the world that he is fact. Notorious for trying to prove his worthiness, he has been known to create counterfeit magazine covers. Time Magazine's editors had to verify that the March 1, 2009, cover of the magazine did not feature a photo of Trump. He falsified the cover to impress his friends, himself, and his club members. The tag suggested that "The Apprentice is a television smash!" Time Magazine's writers are much more creative than that. Mastering the art of the superlative is Thug's strength, but tragically he often projects a pre-school pettiness. The March 2009 cover was fake news and he created it.

Sophomoric denial occasionally kicks in when he conveniently forgets or tosses an appointee under the bus. Matthew Whitaker was appointed acting Attorney General by President Thug, but he doesn't remember meeting him. Whitaker was AG from November 7, 2018, to February 14, 2019, during the

Trump administration.

Teenagers can spread rumors quickly through school. But president Thug is meaner than the cruelest of children at multiplying lies based on malice, emptiness, and pain. "I heard it today that she [Kamala Harris] doesn't meet the requirements," Trump said. "I have no idea if that's right. I would have thought, I would have assumed, that the Democrats would have checked that out before she gets chosen to run for vice president," said President Thug.

How sinister is it to know the truth, spread the lie, and receive approval from your base that the lie is true? Cultic and evil. But here is a list of fraudulent, misleading, and deceptive claims and actions from President Thug, his family, and staff:

- "I never said the pandemic was a Hoax! "Who would say such a thing?"
- "I was opposed to more testing because it reveals more cases."
- "The deep state, or whoever, over at the FDA is making it very difficult for drug companies to get people in order to test the vaccines and therapeutics."
- He always claims to be under audit. "The White House response is that he's not

going to release his tax returns…we litigated this all through the election. People didn't care. They voted for him," said Kellyanne Conway.

- Trump denied climate change. He uses the term "weather extremes" instead of "climate change."

- Unidentified applicants nominated Trump for the Nobel Peace Prize. Two forged nominations were forwarded to the Oslo police for investigation. Authorities believe that both forgeries may have been sent by one source.

- Melania (Melanija Knavs) Trump miraculously received an H-1B visa that allowed her to work in the United States for 5 years. She got an EB-1 "Einstein visa." EB-1 is for applicants who are highly intelligent, skilled, and highly acclaimed in their field such as academic researchers, multinational executives, elite athletes, major prize winners including the Pulitzer, Oscar, Grammy, and Olympic medalists. Melania was no super-model and her EB-1 application cannot be found. She was a model who agreed to be photographed nude, she dated Trump, and she got to the United States in a thinly veiled scheme. I've never been a fan of a first lady having to pose nude in a previous life. Melania Thug is the most nefarious gamer of chain migration. She clearly lacked the talent to obtain an EB-1 on her own merit of definitive talent. Super model? Melania was clearly not in the same league as Iman, Beverly Johnson, Naomi Cambell, Naomi Sims, Kate Moss, Cindy Crawford, Tyra Banks, Ashley Graham, or Donyale Luna. Out of 1 million green cards granted the year Melania arrived, she was in the top 1% exhibiting "extraordinary status." Her parents (Amalija and Viktor Knavs) entered the States by hitching onto Melania and Donald. For the Trump family to be so hard on immigrants, they sure gave grace when family members needed citizenship. Privilege is priceless.

- President Thug eliminated an ethics course for incoming White House staff.
- President Thug cancels White House visitor logs.

- The sister of Jared Kushner, Nicole Kushner Meyer, aka "EB-5 Visa Gate Meets Emoluments," made a bold and ethically-challenged announcement. She was marketing a Kushner-owned property. An ad for the event/investment opportunity, held at a Ritz-Carlton hotel in Beijing, said "Invest $500,000 and immigrate to the United States." For President Thug's family, it's always an opportunity for "Pay-to-Play" and "Pay-to-Vacay."

- President Thug lied about forgetting the name of fallen U.S. Army Sgt. La David Johnson. Gold Star widow, Myeshia Johnson, said, "he couldn't remember my husband's name. If my husband is out here fighting for our country, and he risked his life for our country, why couldn't you remember his name." President Thug lashed back on Twitter saying he had said the sergeant's name throughout the conversation. Myeshia Johnson did not agree.

- After forgetting to contact Gold Star families, President Thug (embarrassed by the mistake) quickly rushed letters via UPS to the families. He previously said that he had contacted "virtually all" Gold Star families.

- Fraud is President Thug's trump card.

10

TREACHERY - LOVE FOES / BETRAY FRIENDS
CIRCLE OF HELL 9

The bottom of Hell is Circle 9 – Treachery. Lucifer sits in Cocytus, the river of frozen tears, located at the lowest level of Hell. The most notorious traitors in history are here -- Brutus, Cassius, Judas Iscariot, John Wilkes Booth, Benedict Arnold, and William Bruce Mumford. While their souls can't escape, Lucifer chews on them forever for their betrayal of trust, their denial of paradise, and for exercising treachery to all good ideas, people, and forms. President Thug seems confused as his body shivers from the extremely cold temperatures. He sees bodies in slush, on ledges, and trapped solid on ice shelves, near Lucifer.

President Thug asks, "Why am I here? Why is it

freezing here? Are we in a simulator? Isn't it supposed to be hot here?"

Dante and Virgil snicker at President Thug, answering snidely, "No, Mr. President, this is not a simulator. This is fire and ice. You are … in Hell."

Dante and Virgil lecture Donald, "You have betrayed family, friends, and followers, Mr. Trump, and your fate may leave you trapped in blocks of ice near Lucifer's jaws for eternity. You have led others away from good; you have twisted the truth and have broken trust. This is where you will see your life, moment by moment. You will witness how the Father of 45,000 lies fleeced, finagled, phished, and fooled friends, flunkies, fawners, and followers into the fiery flames and irritating icicles of Dante's Inferno. Mr. Trump, your earthly obsession with Hell has led you to Hell."

The traitors' bodies in Circle 9 are twisted and uncomfortably contorted in this prison, locked permanently in ice, feeling incessant intermittent frostbite and burning. Lucifer overseas this circle, nibbling and roaring at the damned.

President Thug's treachery is on display in the following examples:

- Trump's own sister, Maryanne Trump Barry said, "You can't trust him. His g**damned tweet[ing] and lying, oh my God. I'm talking too freely, but you know. The change of stories. The lack of preparation. The lying. Holy s***."

- After being impeached, Thug tweeted, **"THIS IS AN ASSAULT ON AMERICA AND AN ASSAULT ON THE REPUBLICAN PARTY!!!!** The tweet never mentioned his actions and the reasons for his impeachment.

- He thinks tearing and shredding papers is legal. He didn't realize that the Presidential Records Act forbids him of destroying all official documents, and any document the President touches is an official document. President Thug's staffers had to meticulously tape the items together to preserve historical integrity and for the President's own legal standing. I guess he thought Enron and Arthur Andersen shredding tactics were legal in the White House.

- While President Obama was placing

sanctions on Russia, Jared Kushner, Michael Flynn, and Russian Ambassador Sergey Kislyak met at Trump Tower to discuss a "line of connection." This whispers treason — the sharing of sensitive American information, and bargaining. Where were the translators? Where are the English transcripts of the conversations? Jeff Sessions also met with Kislyak and Russian diplomats, never mentioning the meetings in his hearings while denying all Trump surrogate conversations. He used campaign funds for the trips. President Thug's campaign was in contact with Russian officials at least 18 times. Kislyak was on the end of several calls. Subterfuge was in full effect.

- President Trump has gone to extraordinary lengths to conceal details of his conversations with Russian President Vladimir Putin. Thug took possession of the notes of his own interpreter and instructed the linguist not to discuss what had transpired with other administration officials (Washington Post).

- President Thug said that he would take

information from a foreign entity about an opponent's campaign. "It's not an interference, they have information - I think I'd take it."

- Thug has always associated himself with questionable business people. Paul Manafort (Thug's former campaign manager) accepted $10 million annually from Russian billionaire, Oleg Deripaska (a close associate to Vladimir Putin). The two had a dispute over $18.9 million, and later, Deripaska accused Manafort of fraud, pledging to recoup the funds.

- President Thug has knowingly shared highly classified information with Russian and North Korean officials. Only those worthy of treason would do this.

- While foreign enemies were exploiting weaknesses in the American Presidency, President Thug downplayed the Russian connection as well as the devastation of Covid-19 on the U.S. He said repeatedly that the virus would disappear suddenly. Several hundred thousand lives later, he contracts Covid-19, and then brags about his supposed miraculous healing and immunity.

- As a "Manchurian candidate turned President," Thug has been lapdog to Vladimir Putin. Dormant for years as a sleeper agent, President Thug acquired prominence and proximity to powerful people. But he was a spy, placed in a target country (his own) not to undertake an immediate mission but to act as a potential asset if activated. His activation came in winning the U.S. Presidency. But the ultimate treason-filled statements by Trump occurred when Trump tried to deflect. "They think it's Russia; I have President Putin, he just said it's not Russia. I will say this: I don't see any reason why it would be. I have great confidence in my intelligence people, but I will tell you that President Putin was extremely strong and powerful in his denial today." The Kremlin had infiltrated and foreign countries realized that Trump was a perfect stooge to put Kompromat in high gear. Russia has damaging information on President Thug, and to cover the blackmail and extortion, Thug hides under Putin's coat for protection. The land of propaganda has captured and activated its pawn.

- Donald Trump is a traitor and his treachery has been discovered.

11

PRIDE - I'LL NEVER APOLOGIZE

PURGATORIO SLICE 1

The Tower of Babel meets Pride and the Trump Tower of Babble. President Thug is obsessed with self. His name must be on everything. The very embodiment of President Thug's insecurity and pride is in his name. He is a man who wants to take credit for everything positive, even if he had nothing to do with it. He never takes blame for failure. Pride comes first, but beware the fall.

- Rhetorical hubris flooded the conversation when Trump asked Kristi Noem, "Do you know it's my dream to have my face on Mount Rushmore?"
- To mimic Xi Jinping, the President of the People's Republic of China, Trump

wanted to abolish term limits. "[Xi's] now president for life. President for life...I think it's great. Maybe we'll have to give that a shot someday."

- Referring to the pandemic, President Thug's lack of care was evident in his quote, "They are dying. That's true. It is what it is."

- Placing his brand and name first and foremost, Thug claimed that he never knew civil rights leader, John Lewis, by saying, "I really don't know [how he will be remembered]. I don't know. I don't know John Lewis. He chose not to come to my inauguration."

- Always wanting to feel like an intelligent, valuable, and purposeful person, President Thug started his own school. It was not accredited, and to graduate, students were forced to give good reviews or risk not getting their bogus certificates. He charged $1,500 to $35,000 for the seminars, which were counterfeit, having no accredited value of knowledge. The school had no meaningful ways to measure student success: no rubrics, no standards, no accredited assessments. Trump said he handpicked the instructors, but testified in a deposition that he never chose the instructors for the program. The instructors weren't even real estate professionals; they were sales sharks. More than 3,500 lawsuits against Trump University levied and leveled the phony school. Saying he would never settle the case, the prideful Thug paid $25 million to settle the fraudulent actions and statements.

- Trump said Hurricane Dorian would pulverize Alabama. The National Weather Service disagreed. Not to be upstaged by scientists and meteorologists, President Thug initiated *Sharpie Gate*, charting his own path for Dorian. The national weather service said Dorian would go no where near Alabama. He was insulted and embarrassed so he had to invent and maintain a story originating from misinformation and pride. This is a thug move like no other. He was wrong and created a narrative of lies to save face. A black Sharpie in the hands of an incompetent and evil man caused chaotic fear in Alabama. He never apologized for the immature action.

- President Thug was surrounded by numerous presidents and prime ministers during a tour of the architecture at NATO. It was not a "Be Best" moment. President Thug heard the cameras clicking. With leaders getting more attention, Thug retaliated. Dusko Markovic, the prime minister of Montenegro, was in the way. President Thug strong-armed him with a right hand to Markovic's right bicep, then forcefully shoved him to the left, while never making eye contact. Thug only looked at the cameras, and had no regard for the other leaders. Melania Trump's anti-bullying campaign doesn't apply to the pride-filled, envious man-child in the White House. Pride goeth before the fall.

12

ENVY - I RESENT YOU AND I'M JEALOUS
PURGATORIO SLICE 2

Obama Envy has become "a thing" with President Thug. He resents the former Commander in Chief on more levels than the Inferno. Every good thing President Obama produced leads to President Thug's bitter indignation. The Affordable Care Act and Obama Envy take up massive residency in Trump's limited mind space. President Thug was a failure at writing a health care bill and his American Health Care Act did not secure guaranteed insurance benefits for patients with pre-existing conditions.

Thug doesn't seek improvement for himself; he only seeks the degradation of others who have paid dues, studied more, saved and earned more money, and have achieved Ivy League status with no aster-isks. His envy morphs to jealousy, and quickly to rage. President Thug knows his mental aptitude is inferior to most people, but denies it by yelling, tweeting, lying, and repeating.

- Trump is afraid of Black women, especially smart, competent, and powerful Black women who can steal attention away from his nonsense. His name calling heightens when Kamala Harris is in the vicinity. He called her the "meanest, most horrible, most disrespectful of anybody in the U.S. Senate."

- How shallow can you be to remove a rule to limit shower heads to 2.5 gallons per minute? President Thug, envious of President Obama's rule on saving water, said, "So shower heads — you take a shower, the water doesn't come out...You want to wash your hands, the water doesn't come out. So what do you do? You just stand there longer or you take a shower longer? Because my hair — I don't know about you, but it has to be perfect. Perfect." Doesn't he know how much 2.5 gallons per minute can emit? He cares more about his ridiculous hair than

saving our most precious resource —
water.

- President Thug said over 150 times that he
  passed the Veteran's Choice law. He
  didn't. The law was passed by Barack
  Obama. Journalist Paula Reid asked him
  repeatedly why he took the credit and he
  angrily and abruptly ended the press
  conference in frustration.

- Absolute power corrupts in an absolute
  way, but President Thug was envious and
  enraged when Sen. John McCain chose to
  keep the Affordable Care Act and to strike
  down the Republican repeal. History was
  made when McCain, in Roman emperor
  fashion, put the "thumbs down" signal on
  Thug's wishes. Once again, Thug was
  shamed by the prisoner of war who risked
  his life for this country. Thug's words
  came back to bite him, "He's not a war
  hero. He was a war hero because he was
  captured. I like people who weren't
  captured." It is clear that President Thug
  envies service vets. He cannot fathom the
  sacrifice; he and his father arranged four
  student deferments so little Donald

wouldn't have to go to war. Thug was cowardly, so his family and doctors created the "bone spur foot scam," while Donald still made claims of being a great athlete. To this day, the doctor's diagnosis is nowhere to be found — mysterious. John McCain deserves accolades for standing up to the bully.

- Testing the waters of followers and sycophants early in his administration, President Thug and his team concocted a lie that the Trump Inauguration had greater attendance than the Obama Inauguration. It wasn't true by head count, evidence in photos, and public declaration. Sean Spicer played to an audience of one and had to declare repeatedly that Trump had more attendees. He had to appease his boss. Spicer and Kellyanne Conway would cling to the term, "alternative facts." Conway, McEnany, Spicer, and Sarah Huckabee Sanders have all succumbed to the manipulation and threats from President Thug.

- The expression "Be Best" is awkward, but Melania didn't know any better. She didn't have a team around her who cared enough to check that the expression is hardly used in English. Why didn't her team correct her? Michelle Obama's expression, "Be Better," was remixed and hijacked by the Trumps, turning it into "Be Best." This is a trait of the Thugs — they are mockingbirds who take what isn't theirs, give it a paint job, and affix their names to the stolen items. Melania Thug stole Michelle Obama's speeches, expressions, and platforms, claiming them as her own. "Your word is your bond." Envy runs strong.

- The Obama Administration proposed that internet companies should offer internet services and cell phones for under $10.00 per month. President Thug wanted to dismantle such an idea. During the Trump administration, 2.3 million people lost their Lifeline phone service and limited internet access. This was cruelty with no regard for the poor.

- The Thug family has been jealous of the Obama family for over a decade. President Thug cannot understand how a Black husband and wife could acquire so much education and success in such a short time. Michelle Obama earned a law degree from Harvard and a sociology degree from Princeton. She became an associate attorney at Sidley Austin, practicing intellectual property and marketing law, a vice-president at University of Chicago Hospital, and First Lady of the United States. She is the bestselling author of the book, *Becoming*. Barack Obama holds a law degree from Harvard (Magna cum Laude) and a political science degree from Columbia. He was a civil rights attorney, Illinois State Senator, United States Senator, and President of the United States. His books, *Dreams from My Father, The Audacity of Hope*, and *A Promised Land*, were all bestsellers. The Obamas also own a film production company, Higher Ground Productions. President Thug has Obama Envy and had the nerve to call the Obamas "grossly incompetent."

- Offering opportunities for young ladies to have educational access throughout the world, Michelle Obama's "Let Girls Learn" initiative was stomped out and defunded by President Thug and Melania Thug.

- Nobel Peace Prize envy is aggravating to President Thug. He has solicited and coerced unknown individuals to nominate him. And he feels Obama didn't deserve one.

- After President Thug found out that federal employees were automatically enrolled and entitled to IRAs, he moved quickly to strike down the Obama law.

- The Colin Kaepernick kneeling exercise was far more than just flags and patriotism. Trump fancies himself as a former athlete (before bone spurs), and he envies the power, prowess, and grace of world class football athletes. Irritation and aggravation intensified because the NFL executives never voted to welcome him into the exclusively prestigious rarified air of NFL team principalship. He doesn't own an NFL team and this infuriates him. Former NFL commissioner Pete Rozelle said, "He was *persona non grata*, too, with the NFL and as long as I or my heirs are involved in the NFL, you will *never* be a franchise owner in the league." So years later, President Thug carries the grudge and says, "Get that son of a bitch off the field right now, he's fired. He's fired!"

- Trump has always been jealous of John McCain. After McCain died, President Thug was so cruel, he only left flags at half-mast for the minimum time required by law.

- President Thug couldn't believe that teenage TikTok users gamed him in Tulsa by securing thousands of tickets to the event, which limited true MAGA supporters from signing up. The event only had 6,600 followers, and the venue was echoing and hollow. TikTok, ya' don't stop.

13

SLOTH - LIFE AS A LAZY TYRANT
PURGATORIO SLICE 3

P resident Thug is lazy. Need I say more? After 3 months in office, he said, "I thought this would be easier." He assumed being President of the United States was an easy job — like starting Trump University, performing half a dozen bankruptcies, manipulating greedy lawyers, producing Miss USA Pageants, and stealing money from family members.

During the California wildfires, we witnessed the classic laziness and sloth of President Thug. He told scientists and researchers, "I don't think that science knows." He obviously doesn't know that the word science means "to know."

He's not a thinker, not a reader, watches 10 hours of TV everyday (too much for any President), ignored his daily briefings, and makes repeated unfound statements. He even hired a PR firm to spin his laziness as "executive time." President Thug spends 92 hours per week in leisure and non-business related activities (watching TV, golfing, and using social media). The average American works 40-50 hours per week. There are only 168 hours in a week. When did he have time to be President? During his first year in office, he signed the fewest pieces of legislation for any president since Eisenhower.

The Department of Education sent out a tweet misspelling one of America's greatest scholars.

"Education must not simply teach work - it must teach life." – W.E.B. <u>DeBois</u> [sic]. DuBois is the correct spelling. The Department of Education later misspelled the word "apologizes" for which they later apologized for spelling it "apologies." This was sent by the unqualified and laughable Betsy DeVos, Secretary of Education.

Trump has had a terrible firing record and resignation turnover. He has lost 91 handpicked members in executive offices. The last four presidents were 20% lower. Trump's cabinet turnover number was 10, which was more than the last 5 presidents, and 20% more than George H.W. Bush. This shows that President Thug lacks a penchant for effectively hiring good people for specific roles. His laziness became clear when administrative responsibilities began to disintegrate.

But always trying to prove that he is a smart person who is mentally astute and sharp, he chirped these words as effectively as a talking parrot. Trump bragged about repeating five words, during a cognitive test.

"Person. Woman. Man. Camera. TV."

"Could you repeat that?"

"Yeah. It's Person. Woman. Man. Camera. TV."

"They say, 'That's amazing. How did you do that?'"

"I do it because I have, like, a good memory, because I'm cognitively there."

He could have added one more word to his list: Sloth. Why did the press cover this man's grandiosity of word play? It gets worse.

Instead of doing a major search for a qualified professional with housing and urban development experience, President Thug chose laziness and racism by appointing a world renown retired neurosurgeon to be the Secretary of HUD. Dr. Ben Carson had no housing experience, had more concerns for his office décor, and treated low-income housing with little priority.

President Thug speaks at a fourth-grade level, the

lowest of the last 19 presidents. Boston Globe reporter Matt Viser showed how this limitation became an advantage for Thug, understood more quickly by MAGA, who Thug calls, "the poorly educated." He is ignorant, lazy, and deliberate in his shallow delivery. Speech specialists agree that "Republican candidates — like Trump — who are speaking at a level easily understood by people at the lower end of the education spectrum [outperform] their highfalutin opponents in the polls. Simpler language resonates with a broader swath of voters in an era of 140-character Twitter tweets and 10-second television sound bites."

President Thug spells "hamberger" with an "e" and "Nobel Prize" as "Noble Prize." It's novel and noble for him to mention that he would like a Nobel Prize, but for now his spelling, syntax, and pronunciation all prove to be nightmares. Thug knows that the detailed expression of sounding "presidential" and intelligent doesn't serve him well. He plays it down. Pronouncing Yosemite, as "Yo-suh-might" during a speech on national parks was brutal. How can an American President mispronounce Yosemite National Park?

President Thug decided to not renew contracts for individuals on the EPA's Advisory Board. He also appointed campaign workers to the Department of Agriculture, but none of them obtained a college degree in the field of agriculture.

President Thug is too lazy to remain in work environments. He enjoys time at his own residences and resorts. He spends 1 out of every 3 days away from the White House, avoiding work, searching for golfing opportunities, and dismissing his daily briefings. He enjoys the title but hates the responsibilities.

President Thug's record is the greatest indicator that sloth has had damaging effects on the United States.

14

PARADISO LOST
EYE OF A NEEDLE

P resident Thug does not desire Paradiso. He loathes honesty, fortitude, good works, spiritual love, theology, thoughtfulness, blessedness, and virtue. His soul is counterfeit and empty, devoid of love for anyone other than Donald J. Trump.

The Republican Party, Cambridge Analytica, the Russian government, the Electoral College, Breitbart, Fox News, Facebook, Twitter, MAGA, and Trump supporters fostered and committed grave acts when they created a pathway for the election of a debased and horrible human being.

President Thug needs to repent and apologize for his destructive behavior. He needs to seek Paradiso. If not, he can continue to be at peace with his place in Dante's Inferno.

CREDITS AND REFERENCES

Thanks to the courageous journalists who risk their time, reputation, and lives to get us the story. They deserve more respect, more money, and to not be called fake news. We value their sacrifice and tireless efforts to research, write, edit, and meet deadlines. Endless applause to those who embrace the life of journalism. God's blessings and Paradiso to:

Yamiche Alcindor, Dante Alighieri, AlterNet.org, Associated Press, The Atlantic, BallotReady.org, Michael Biesecker, Peter Beinart, Russ Buettner, Boston Globe, Bournemouth University, Jonathan Capehart, James Carville, Francesca Chambers, Chicago Tribune, Chicago Sun Times, The Circus, City University of New York, David Choi, Christianity Today, Keith Collins, The Conversation, CNN,

Susanne Craig, Sophia DuRose, John Ehle, Rehema Ellis, David Fahrentold, Marc Fisher, Fox News, Michael Francis, Kevin Freking, Mark Galli, Sophie Gilbert, Jeffrey Goldberg, Richard Grusin, Robert O'Harrow Jr., Jemele Hill, Karen Hunter, I Am Your Target Demographic, Jason Johnson, Journal of Language and Politics, Brian Klaas, Steve Kornacki, Michael Kranish, Ramona Kreis, Adrienne LaFrance, Jonathan Lemire, Don Lemon, The Lincoln Project, Rachel Maddow, Roland Martin, Jeff Mason, McSweeney's Internet Tendency, Mike McIntire, John McMurtrie, Medium Magazine, Chris Monks, MSNBC, Amanda Mull, NBC News, New York Times, Weijia Jiang, The New Yorker, Alex Niemczewski, Caitlin Oprysko, Ben Parker, Joshua Partlow, Abby Phillip, Politico, Politifact, Real Clear Politics, The Reich Wing Republican Joke Page, Joy-Ann Reid, Paula Reid, Barry Richards, Eugene Robinson, Kelsey Ronan, Aviva Rosman, Phillip Rucker, April Ryan, Stephanie Steinbrecher, Amy Sumerton, Sophia Tareen, Time Magazine, Trump's Twitter Account, USA Today, U.S. News & World Report, Cecelia Vega, Rachel Villa, Matt Viser, Vox, Washington Post, Kristen Welker, White House Press Corps, Peter Wehner, and Bob Woodward.

ABOUT THE AUTHOR

Garrard McClendon is a Professor of Education at Chicago State University. He is the author of *Ax or Ask? The African American Guide to Better English,* and the editor of *Donda's Rules: The Scholarly Works of Dr. Donda West (Mother of Kanye West).* He has earned an Emmy Award, the One Region Award, an Associated Press Award, and an NAACP Champion Award. McClendon is the Executive Director of the Milton & Ruby McClendon Scholarship Fund.

f 𝕏 ⃝